The Final Duty Station

David Forrest West

Foreword

The *Philadelphia Inquirer* ran an article on July 23, 1944 announcing the names, age, rank and addresses of the first group of 13 US Marines, all from the First Marine Division, returning to Philadelphia after 25 months of service in the South Pacific. The article acknowledged their role in "liquidating the Japs in the Solomon Islands" and being "awarded the Presidential unit citation." The article however did not explain that these men were the lucky ones having won the rotation lottery where there was a qualified Marine to take their spot in their unit and thus got to transfer back to a "Stateside" assignment and out of harms way.

One of these returnees was my father, Staff Sergeant Wilbert (Bill) Forrest West, 25, of 1519 Blavis St. This is his war story told in the first-person as he speaks directly to his family from *The Final Duty Station* (Heaven to a Marine).

In this account, we witness things as he likely would have experienced them; with his own fears, triumphs, frustrations and everyday personal emotions on the battlefield and off. After the war was finally over he returned to Philadelphia again, this time from the Boston Navy Yard. He married, raised a family, and never again left the place he loved so well.

David Forrest West

Dear Family,   Christmas 2019

January 3, 2019 would have been my 100th Birthday. Christmas was always special for me so I am giving this gift to you, so you may especially remember this year's holiday.

I thought I would use the occasion to tell you a story about my service in the US Marine Corps during World War II. After the War was over I spoke very little about it, as was the case with other veterans of that horrible worldwide conflict. The United States saw over 16 million citizen-soldiers serve in the Military and over 407 thousand of them would perish.

It was complicated for me, because how could I describe things that I saw and heard, that unless you were there you could never, ever comprehend the horrors. And besides I didn't necessarily want to relive those events with some old geezers at a VFW hall or at Marine Corps reunions. That just wasn't my way. So I just repressed it and went about the business of living my life as a civilian that was proud to have served his country as a Marine during such a historic time.

I now regret not sharing more of these experiences with David and Deborah while I could. I know they would've been wide-eyed and very interested in hearing my "war stories." I hope you will appreciate this piece of family legacy and pass it down to future generations so that it remains in the family.

Contents

Chapter 1

Why the Marines?

One of the biggest influences on me as a child was finding my Uncle Charlie's old Marine Dress Blue uniform in the closet at my Grandparent's house on North Eleventh Street in Philadelphia. When I was twelve years old, around the year 1931, I would sneak upstairs and put his uniform on and look in the mirror imagining being a Marine one day. My Uncle was short, only five and a half feet, so the uniform fit me pretty well. After my war was over, anytime I would see Marines in their Dress Blues I would get a proud tear in my eye because of what that uniform represents. The very best!

Charles Augustus Straka was my Dad's younger brother and only sibling. He was a rough and tumble type of guy, just the opposite of my father. He enlisted in The Marines in 1918 at the age of 27, hoping to get in on the World War I action over in France as a *Devil Dog* fighting the Germans. Instead he was sent to The Dominican Republic when President Wilson decided to send in *The Marines* in a peace-keeping mission to stabilize the government there. My Uncle never did take the *West* surname and his military records showed that as a Private, Charles Straka; "engaged the Dominican bandits in the hills around the Capital of Santiago." He was discharged from the Marines at the end of 1919.

Another example of patriotic service was from my Grandmother Young's family who came over from Germany. Those ancestors immigrated to Pennsylvania back in the mid-eighteen century as farmers and many of them proudly fought in militias during *The Revolutionary War* and *The Civil War*.

Another uniform I got to wear was as a *Boy Scout of America*. At age 14, I joined BSA Troop #238 in Philadelphia. We did all the typical Boy Scout activities and camping trips which I believe also led to my interest in becoming a Marine.

At NorthEast Public High School I was on the Varsity Swim Team for three years and became quite good in long distance swimming. I also liked playing football and other physically demanding sports. My nickname was "Bud."

As soon as I turned sixteen years old I was allowed to join The Philadelphia Rifle Club in 1935. Rifle clubs in major cities were a strong cultural tradition brought over from Germany. Young boys were taught how to properly use firearms to hunt with, which in the old country, helped put food on their family's table. They also served as social organizations within the German community. In the summer months the Club would hold picnics every Sunday afternoon in the East Falls section of Fairmont Park with hundreds in attendance. The Club's rifle range was in our old Olney neighborhood. By the time I enlisted I had a half-dozen years experience with rifles and was already rated as "an expert marksman."

Chapter 2

Enlistment & Boot Camp

After graduating high school I attended The Charles
Morris Price School of Advertising & Journalism for three
years. That education afforded me the chance to begin work
in the field of marketing and advertising for Donavan &
Armstrong & Co. for two years before enlisting.

During this time period, around the dinner table, there
was much discussion about the pros and cons of the United
States entering the war. I decided I wanted to enlist rather
than wait to be drafted into the Army or some other fate not
of my own choosing.

After discussing it with my parents and older sister
Mildred, I set out to explore my options. My Mother was the
most concerned as you might imagine. In late summer of 1941
I visited Uncle Sam's Recruiting Offices on Broad Street and
talked to both the Navy and Marine Corps recruiting officers.
Once again it was those damn *Dress Blue Uniforms* that
swayed my decision. Down deep I always knew I wanted to be
a Marine. So my Recruiter gave me the date of 5 September
1941, right after the Labor Day Holiday, to return to their
office ready to go to Parris Island, South Carolina. First, I
would have to pass their basic physical exam. I was worried

that my flat feet might disqualify me, but in the end it did not. I had a very short time to get my affairs in order and say goodbye to my family and friends.

As it turned out my enlistment would come only three months before *Pearl Harbor's Day of Infamy.*

That September morning I gave my oath to "defend my country" as a recruit in the US Marine Corps and was immediately assigned to "Active Duty." My travel orders, along with several other recruits, were already prepared to have us travel directly by train from Philadelphia and arrive at Boot Camp on the Marine bus. Uncle Sam generously gave each of us *one dollar* for "subsistence en-route." I used my dollar to buy a couple of Coca-Colas and some candy bars.

Boot Camp at Parris Island, South Carolina

I was 22 years old and now a lowly *boot* at one of toughest camps to survive in the military. A camp that has been training Marines since 1891. This experience would be a rite of passage that would mold me into "Marine Manhood."

South Carolina was terribly hot, humid and infested with biting bugs, snakes and other creatures not found in Pennsylvania. Not to mention home of a unique specimen of man wearing a funny looking *Smokey The Bear* hat. That man was a really nasty 'S.O.B' of a Drill Instructor (DI), whose job it was to whip our baby smooth asses into shape.

Boy Scout Wilbert Forrest West in 1933

NorthEast High School Graduation 1937

After a grueling two day train trip on the *B&O Line* and a long bus ride to the camp, the first thing we heard shouted at us when we arrived was: "NOW,GET OFF MY BUS." We all jumped out of our seats and trampled off of that bus as fast as we could. We then quickly fell in line on the tightly stenciled yellow footprints painted on the concrete sidewalk as we were ordered by the DI. I was shaking in my shoes standing there.

The next thing you know is that organized chaos is about to be thrust on you for a whirlwind 72 hours of receiving, or in-processing. We all lined up for our medical exams, inoculations, buzz-cuts that they call "high and tight." We then go through an assembly type line for getting all of our provisions from the various store rooms of uniforms, equipment and other gear needed for the next ten weeks. We also had to take an initial strength test, which I passed easily.

I was assigned to be part of Platoon 136 with 60 other recruits. This platoon was one of 6 others making up Delta Company; The First Recruit Training Battalion. There were approximately 1,500 recruits in the Battalion. Our motto was *"Ab Uno Disce Fidelis"* or *"From the First come Faithfulness."* Our Drill Instructor was Sergeant E. B. McNeil from New England. He would poke fun at my name, Wilbert, by comically shouting out "Wiiilll- Burrt" real loud. He knew that would get under my skin because I wanted to be called

Bill, not Wilbert. Our DI was assisted by a PFC Holmes who would chuckle under his breath at the whole "Wilbert" thing.

One of the first things we learned to do were *close order drills* with our rifle. Our platoon drilled on the large Parade Deck almost non-stop and it really did help mold us into a close-nit unit. During the initial weeks we learned about the Marine Corps history, core values, customs and how to properly wear the uniform. We also learned about basic first aid, hand-to-hand combat and a variety of Marine adapted Martial Arts. One of which was the "choke hold" which was to disable and /or kill an enemy. We trained constantly, six days a week, with Sunday's off for rest and religious services. We were also always expected to be ready for "close inspection" of our bunks and foot-lockers, our uniforms and our weapons.

PI Boot Camp Platoon 136 November 1941

Boot Camp really was an indoctrination into a new lifestyle. We had to relearn everything we thought we knew into *The Marine Way*. We had to refer to ourselves in the third person, such as "this recruit." There was also a new language to learn. Hats were covers, green T-shirts were Skivvy Shirts, food was chow, etc. We even were taught the proper way to clean ourselves in the showers. The essence of all this was to psychologically break down the recruit from being an individual and then rebuild them back up as part of the unit. If any one of us screwed up, we all screwed up. We were often given 'IT' or "incentive training" by the DI. This could be anything from push-ups to hikes with our rifle carried above our heads for the whole platoon or just one recruit. Most used response to the DI was: "SIR, YES SIR."

One of the things that helped me through a lot of these physical and mental challenges was I kept telling myself over and over that; "I was going to make it through to the end or I was going to die, there was no quitting." During our four plus mile "motivation runs" around Parris Island we would "sound off" with various rhyming jingles to keep our minds off the physical pain and to stay motivated.

We would shout as we ran:

Feels good Like it should Feels fine Double time!

Week Four started to go better, it was *Swim Week,* which is as basic as it can get for a Marine. We learned how to undress under water, tread water for long periods and make long swims in the ocean. I passed all of this easily, but there were some recruits that; believe it or not, did not know how to swim. They had a very bad week.

Week Five was *Team Week*. Half-way through, and we got a short break from the non-stop training. Instead we worked around the camp doing clean-up of the grounds, helping in the supply warehouses and what ever else we were told to do.

Week Six was called *Grass Week*. It was focused on the basics of handling our rifle in the field. We were taught all the various positions out on the rifle range and then practicing them in hidden spots around the base. *Week Seven* was similar to last week, but now we were given live ammunition to shoot with at various distances. We were expected to hit a target at 100 yards, and also trained for targets up to 500 yards.

During these weeks our platoon took long hikes in the mid-day heat on Saturdays going 5-6 miles, sometimes with full packs and rifles. At least we had Sundays to recover.

Week Eight was called *"Basic Warrior Training"* when we were expected to perform assault and attack drills over various terrains, including amphibious beach landings. Hand - to-Hand combat exercises in water, sand and mud were also a part of this training. This week was the most brutal by far.

Week Nine was *Testing*. This was a week's worth of physical and mental tests of what we had been taught the previous eight weeks. This recruit had already passed the pistol test and was rated as a *marksman* with the rifle. Testing also included proper hand grenade and bayonet use. For this recruit's last test he passed the bayonet with an excellent score on 10 November 1941 which was The Marine Corps' Birthday. In 1775 the Marines were founded at Tun Tavern in Philadelphia on that day. How fitting that a guy from Philly completed his boot camp also on that day.

Week Ten was *Graduation*. Most of our original platoon of 60 recruits passed the testing with flying colors. We did have a couple of mis-fits that washed out. I had wanted my Dad to come down for the graduation ceremony, but he could not be away from his job, he worked so many hours every week. Being awarded the *Black Eagle, Globe & Anchor* emblem and finally being called "Marine," and no longer being considered a recruit or boot, was one of the proudest moments in my life. This once lowly recruit, Bill West, had what it took and had survived Marine Corps Boot Camp while learning the vaunted *Warrior Ethos* that separated us from all the other fighting forces in the world. Members of Delta Company, Platoon 136, would now split-up and transfer to other Marine bases for further training.

Quartermaster (QM) School - Philadelphia

Each recruit was told to consider what they wanted to specialize in after boot camp. Those that did not have a preference would be assigned to a rifle platoon or another combat platoon such as mortars and machine guns based on what was needed. Those that had certain skills and had a specific non-combat job in mind could put a request in writing to the commanding general. I had learned that the Marine QM school was in Philadelphia. For sure that was a big reason for my request to be back home, but I also strongly believed it fit my personality along with the administrative skills learned in high school and in the advertising and journalism business. I liked attention to detail and keeping track of things. On 6 November, I formally requested transfer to the QM School. On 17 November 1941 General A. A. Vandegrift's Office in Washington approved my request.

I prepared everything I needed in order to leave Parris Island on 22 November and take the train back home to Philadelphia. After graduation, I had waited patiently in camp until I got the reply for my transfer. I also killed time with some of my buddies and we would usually head into town at night. Every town with a Marine Base has some sort of watering hole and fun adult stuff to offer up including many available single women. Parris Island was no different.

Private Bill West January, 1942 at QM School, Philadelphia

I had not been home in eleven weeks, which was the longest I had ever been away from home, and I was honestly a little homesick. My family was thrilled I was coming back home, at least for a while. I returned for my proud parents to see me in uniform as a newly minted Marine Corps' Private.

I was ordered to report to The Marine Barracks at The Philadelphia Navy Yard on 23 November to begin QM school. Philadelphia was already a major military supply and logistics hub so it made sense that The Marine Corps had their school located there. It was also where most all of the military uniforms were produced with the skilled immigrant women and textile equipment near the Navy Base in South Philadelphia. The first two weeks were pretty routine learning the basic procedures for ordering and dispersing supplies and equipment. I even had weekend leave, and just in time for Thanksgiving, to see family and friends and sleep in my own bed again on Blavis Street. My brother Walt had started college at Lehigh University so I would not get to see him until Christmas.

However, after the sneak attack on Pearl Harbor on 7 December 1941 and with the United States officially entering the war, a lot changed as you would imagine. Being at a major Naval Base we worried that we might be attacked next, if not from the Japs, then maybe German U-boats. Security tightened around the base and black-out precautions were taken. The US Navy was reeling from the loss of so many ships at Pearl Harbor and the news that the Imperial Japanese Navy continued to strike at more Allied bases in the Pacific was definitely more reason for concern. It truly became "all hands on deck" around the base. Leaves were cancelled and certain reserve units were being called up. Philadelphia was a major ship building center back then and almost immediately the call for more ships to be built went out from the War Department. The Navy Yard soon after started to build their next Battleship, the *USS New Jersey.*

A lot of my friends from high school and around the neighborhood called my parents wanting to talk to me about signing up with *The Marines.* Almost everyone felt the patriotic sense of duty to help win the war. As Christmas 1941 approached everyone also wanted to be in a holiday mood, but it became pretty somber when we realized what the next year or even years would be like fighting a world-wide war.

The Quartermaster School was a ten-week program which I completed on 2 February 1942. With this accomplishment, I received the standard promotion to Private First Class (PFC-E2) which meant another stripe on my uniform and the next higher pay grade.

I had already prepared my parents for the fact that soon after QM school I would have to transfer back down south to New River, North Carolina to join The First Marine Division.

Chapter 3

First Marine Division

The First Marine Division (FMD) was activated on 1 Feb. 1941. This happened aboard a Navy Destroyer after completing landing exercises on the beaches around Guantanomo Bay, Cuba. Thus proving they were capable of their primary mission which is to perform amphibious warfare in significant numbers. They got the nickname of *The Old Breed* after that and their motto was: "No Better Friend, No Worst Enemy."

New River, North Carolina

Prior to finishing QM school I had gotten my orders to report to The Marine Camp in New River. It was the Fleet Marine Force's brand new headquarters built in 1941. It sat on 240 square miles of land with 14 miles of beach along the Atlantic Ocean. This massive property is just about twice the size as the City of Philadelphia. It was a coastal wilderness and very intimidating with swamps and jungle like terrain.

I took the next train out of 30th Street Station and arrived 3 February 1942. I was assigned to Headquarter's Battalion of this newly activated First Marine Division. The fact that we were in a new base, with a new combat division, the War Department had to have been planning by early 1941 for us to eventually come into the war. I was assigned to a barracks with other Quartermasters and reconnected with many of the Marines from boot camp after they had completed their own specialized training. The purpose of the next several months would be to give us advanced training to become *battle ready* as an amphibious force somewhere against an Axis or Imperial Power. We spent a lot of time practicing and coordinating for beach landings off of transport ships and into *Higgins LCT's* which included climbing down rope cargo ladders. My job was also to train for getting the supplies ashore. On land we drilled, ran obstacle courses, and went on hikes into deep jungle sites to improve our navigation abilities in unfamiliar terrain. Everybody was pretty *"Gung-Ho"* * about the combat training because we knew that it would be for real sometime soon.

*"Gung-Ho" was a Chinese expression meaning "Work Together". It was adopted by Marine Colonel Evans Carlson in WWII as he led a Raider Battalion that trained in Mainland China.

The base, although pretty spartan, did have some nice features. There was a PX, movie theater and an outdoor club area just for privates to relax away from any officers. I liked the PX because I had taken up pipe smoking and that is where I got my tobacco. I would catch a movie on a Saturday with some of my buddies and go to the Protestant Church on Sunday morning. Sunday afternoon was for writing letters.

During the time in New River (later named Camp Lejeune), we had two weekend passes to go home. The first one was Easter in April and the second was in early June just before shipping out. We rounded-up a bunch of guys going up to Philly and hired a local taxi driver to take us straight to Union Station in Washington, DC on Friday. We then caught an evening train. The driver would sleep in his car and wait for us to return late on Sunday and then drive us straight back to the base. We somehow knew that the three day pass on 6 June, 1942 would be our last time home for quite awhile and perhaps, god-forbid, ever. I sensed that my parents knew this potentiality as well. Things had not been going well for the Allies, especially in The Pacific, and something had to be done to stop the Japanese. As I walked down our front steps, it was very emotional to see them crying as I said my good-byes.

The Pentagon's First Plans To Go To War

Around mid-April 1942, just a few months after Pearl Harbor, the War Department had secretly set up a plan to move the FMD in stages to Wellington, New Zealand. It was called operation *Lone Wolf* and it was to commence immediately. An advance team flew directly to Wellington to begin construction of a forward base for us to use in the South Pacific. Then shortly after that elements of our command structure battalion, including General Vandergrift and his staff, boarded the *USS WAKEFIELD* in Norfolk, VA and sailed for the Pacific through the Panama Canal. We later found out that Vandergrift said he needed six-months in New Zealand to get us combat ready. However, that was not even close to being "in the cards."

During these critical weeks on the home front, America had begun converting it's industries to a full out war-time footing. President Roosevelt called America: *"The Arsenal of Democracy"* as he delivered his *Four Freedoms* speech to explain the how and why for winning the war. The FMD would soon realize exactly how unprepared America was as we got called up to be the first ones to challenge the enemy.

We got back to New River on Monday, 8 June and were told that all future leaves were cancelled and to get ready to ship out at a moments notice. We collected our vintage WWI Springfield bolt action rifles, fatigues, sleeping roll, personal gear stuffed into a duffle bag, wrote some letters home and waited and waited. That moment came a few days later when most of the FMD started boarding trains on Saturday, 13 June which soon after started rolling westward. Our destination was *Top Secret* and any "loose lips" could result in court martial. The trains they used were full scale *Pullman Sleeper Cars*, but they assigned two Marines to each berth somewhat uncomfortably. From what we could tell the trains were taking a zig-zag route; going south, then west, then north again. We found out that there were Federal Agents assigned to the train to make sure no one passed information about our whereabouts at the stops we made along the way. One poor fellow was thrown in the brig on the train for talking to a porter. Once we hit the prairie we just stayed on a fast west-bound track and eventually stopped at one of *The Harvey House** locations in Royal Gorge, Colorado. The waitresses there were all really pretty and made us feel special. I wondered to myself if this might be the last time I would see an *American Gal* for a while. Finally on Friday night, 19 June we disembarked our train at San Francisco's Union Station. "My God we are headed out to The Pacific," I said out loud.

* Harvey Houses were famous throughout the West for train travel rest-stops which featured good food served by attractive and friendly waitresses.

Welcome to the USAT JOHN ERICSSON

Military trucks quickly took all of the elements of the rear echelon from the train station over to the Port of Oakland where we boarded our troop transport ship. Our ship was the *USAT JOHN ERICSSON* which had just been requisitioned by the Government from the Swedish American Line. It had sailed under the name of *MS KUNGSHOLM*, a passenger liner built in Germany in 1928. For the next two days I assisted in coordinating the loading of all of the supplies for the convoy before we could set sail. We were told to load enough food and commodities for at least three weeks at sea. I quickly began to get the impression that much of the detailed planning we were taught in QM school was out the window and we were flying by the seat of our pants. It was my first real big "SNAFU"* moment in the Marine Corps.

*SNAFU (Situation Normal All Fouled Up) is one of several Marine Corps acronyms for foul-ups. FUBAR (F***ed Up Beyond All Recognition) and "A Real Cluster F***" are others.

There were another nine ships making up our part of the overall convoy. Some Marines passed the time gambling on ship or going to the USO. Many wrote letters but could not say where they were. Unless they would make the censors do what they do. On Sunday, 22 June 1942 we pushed away from the dock not knowing where we were headed or for how long. I will always remember how I felt sailing under the beautiful Golden Gate Bridge and watching the California coast line disappear as our convoy steamed into the open waters of the Pacific. I saw many a Marine with tears in their eyes as they tried to control the dueling emotions of patriotic excitement and the onset of that proverbial emotion; homesickness.

The first few days at sea were uneventful. Knowing what I saw during loading, I began to worry about the adequacy of our food supply for feeding that many men while on board. After two days at sea we were officially told we would be heading to Wellington, New Zealand to meet-up with the advance units of the FMD. Not many of us knew exactly where New Zealand was, except it was very far away, like halfway around the globe. My fears began to mount about the food supply. I kept remembering the phrase; "An Army marches on its' stomach" and thinking: "My God how can we fight a war without food to keep us strong?" I was just starting to see how poorly prepared we really were to go to war.

The veteran sailors on board ship started reminding the uninitiated Marines about the Ancient Mariner's ritual of *Crossing The Equator* as *Pollywogs* being introduced to the mysteries of the sea kingdom of *Neptunus Rex*. This *time honored tradition* is carried out to test your endurance and see if you can qualify as *"ShellBacks"* by being hazed and humiliated by the other sea-men that have come before. The estimated date for the crossing was 1 July 1942 and we were told that we better prepare. "We were Marines bound for war, yet we had to still endure this crazy Navy crap," is basically how I felt about it. OK, let's get it over with. I survived Boot Camp, I surely can handle this too. Shave my head, paddle my butt, make me run the gauntlet, further humiliate me and then give me a certificate from *"The Ancient Order of the Deep"*. It's now official. I am now a goddam ShellBack!

We still had about ten more days at sea, under the *Southern Cross* sky, until we reached New Zealand and the food situation was worsening. Chicken had turned green with mold and many of the guys had diarrhea, making an overcrowded situation even worse. When we finally reached Wellington on 11 July after 20 days at sea, and a distance of

6,500 nautical miles, the average Marine on board had lost 16 pounds. To add insult to injury, we had to wait until the next day to disembark our hellhole ship. Good riddance *John Ericsson*!

Wellington, NZ: What happened to the Plan?

When we arrived it was already winter and it poured a hard, cold rain almost every day. Our main objective was to get all the equipment and supplies *Combat Ready** for an expected amphibious landing. The FMD's orders were to move into their recently built barracks and complete their combat training over a few more months. A plan that was logical enough. Except, the new orders that came down from *The Pentagon* moved the plan up to days, not months. And by the way, the New Zealand dock workers, that we desperately needed to help us, were on strike. Another major SNAFU was upon us. By the time we started work at the Aotea Quay docks, we only had 10 days to reload everything for combat. So we malnourished Marines all went to work. We had four hour shifts, on and off, around the clock. There were ships coming from the States with supplies that were being unloaded and loaded at the same time. Supplies packed in cardboard boxes melted away in the rain on the open dock.

*Combat Ready is an organized method to insure that supplies and equipment are off loaded as the troops will need them in an amphibious assault.

Despite the insane schedule to get ready to ship out, there were Marines that risked going AWOL and went over the fence to experience Wellington's nightlife and the New Zealand women that they had heard were friendly to Yanks. I did get into town while there and picked up a few coins as souvenirs which I had kept with me throughout the war for good luck. Many credited General Vandergift's leadership style which enabled us to get the job done on schedule. That along with the unofficial motto of *"Improvise, Adapt, and Overcome"* helps explain the Marine Way of solving impossible problems. The troop ship that I would soon be embarking on was the *USS Hunter Liggett*. This ship was a vintage 1922 passenger ship, reconfigured into a Navy attack transport vessel in 1939. She was manned with a Coast Guard crew which had sailed from the Brooklyn Navy Yard and had been waiting in Wellington since the end of May. I was among the 1,500 Marines that boarded her on 22 July and set sail along with a whole flotilla of some 89 ships. In total, 956 officers and 18,146 enlisted men comprised the FMD. Our convoy was practically all the ships in the Pacific fleet at the time. The logistical plan was that we would leave port with a 60 day combat load. We learned we would be headed to Koro Islands off of Fiji for practice landings in the *Higgins Boats.**

*Higgins Boats (LCV's) were the mastermind of Andrew Higgins of New Orleans who designed them to operate in the swamps and marshes of the bayou and were constructed of plywood.

Chapter 4

Operation WatchTower: Halt Japan

The practice maneuvers at Koro Islands were a lost opportunity because no one was aware that the waters near the beaches were all coral and would chew up the bottoms of the *Higgins Boats*, not to mention the Marines going over the side. So eventually those landing exercises were scrubbed and we began heading towards our ultimate objective in the little known British Solomon Islands on 31 July 1942.

The FMD's real mission, which was still secret, was to execute simultaneous landings that would take place on two different islands in the Solomons. The first, on the smaller island of Tulagi where the Japanese Army had established a small fighting force base at the site of the British Consulate , and then at roughly the same time on Guadalcanal where there was an airfield under construction. That airfield when completed would allow the Japanese to control all the shipping lanes down to Australia and New Zealand. The presumption was that the Japanese had significant combat forces protecting the new airfield. Our convoy approached the island chain from the West on 6 August 1942 and during the night sailed up a body of water called *Sealark Channel*. As a possible good omen, our entire fleet went undetected because of heavy cloud cover, whereafter the convoy split-up for the two separate invasions the next day.

Turning Point of the War in the Pacific

This day was going to be America's first amphibious operation since 1898 during The Spanish-American War in Cuba. Also, this was America's first true offensive campaign of WWII. Strategically, morally, emotionally the stakes could not have been higher for our country. The Japanese onslaught in the Pacific had to be stopped and Guadalcanal was literally *"the line in the sand."*

We Had to Win Period!

At sunrise, around 0600 on 7 August, exactly eight months after Pearl Harbor, General Quarters was sounded on our ship, as well as all the other ships in the convoy. Soon after came the specific orders, addressed over the intercom: "stand-by to land." The *Higgins Boats* were being slowly and systematically lowered into the water one by one and the massive naval bombardment from all the Cruiser's large guns commenced in deafening fashion. This lasted until the first wave moved ashore around 0915. I got out of my bunk and began getting dressed in my green utility uniform in a very robotic fashion trying to hide my nervousness to those around me. We were then funneled up to the mess deck for the ritual of Steak & Eggs as the symbolic "last hot meal." In fact many Marines were not able to keep that special meal down once they got going in the landing crafts. A damned waste of a good steak I reckoned.

Climbing down the cargo nets. Courtesy Life Magazine

My turn to go over the side would not come until later. Since I was *Rear Echelon*, or administration and supply, we were not scheduled until the seventh wave much later that morning. By 0910 most of the *Advance Echelon Battalions* were in their *Higgins Boats* and going ashore at what was designated as *Red Beach*.* Word quickly got back to our ship from the coxswains informing the landing officer that little or no resistance was coming from the enemy and there were no shots being fired. We did not know if that meant "Ambush" or "Surrender" or something all together else and more deadly. Intelligence was non-existence until we could get organized ashore. We did hear one funny story about a Marine who

31

somehow injured himself trying to open a coconut with his own K-bar bayonet.

*The Naval Officers would designate their "Landing Zones" (LZ's) and define their colors throughout the war. They would have the authority to decide the best location for the primary safety of their ships, not the Marines. This created conflict and undue loss on Guadalcanal. Since then the rules were changed and the Marine Commander now decides where and when they land. This helped save lives on other island landings during the war.

I made my way up to the starboard deck where we would start to climb down the cargo nets into our designated landing craft. Thankfully there were no wounded Marines coming back from the beaches to offload, because there were none. It was already 1130 and I had started feeling lethargic from the long morning's wait. I was fully packed and loaded with my gear and my lucky orange from breakfast. I finally got the ok to go and with the adrenaline pumping I climbed down the rope cargo net. I was ready to roll. Fifteen minutes later we were headed to our *Red Beach LZ*. Our Higgins boat carried about 35 Marines and was piloted by a single *Coastie* (slang for Coast Guard Private). It made its way to *Red Beach* going about 15 knots. The sea was very calm that day and our *Coastie* was able to get us within 10 yards from the beach where we climbed up on the side of our craft and jumped feet first into the warm tropical water. I said to myself: "Oh shit West, here we go," as I waded the short distance ashore.

Above: The US 1st Marine Division landed on Guadalcanal on August 7, 1942, coming ashore on Red Beach, a 1,500-yards stretch of shore located about four miles to the east of where the Japanese were building their airstrip. The landings were unopposed, but problems developed later in the day when the shore parties could not handle the

First Pioneer Battalion was responsible for "ship-to-shore" movement of supplies.

All of our months of training and preparation was about to be put to the test. Known only to God, those of us that were not killed or wounded, would not be going back aboard any ship for the next nineteen long, long weeks. The advance echelon Marines had cleared the beach and were already headed into the jungle towards a place called the *Grassy Knoll*. There was no resistance to any of our advances inland. Meanwhile supplies and equipment were piling up on the beach as the Navy unloaded the cargo as fast as possible anticipating an attack by air once Rabaul* was notified of the landings.

*Rabaul was the major Japanese forward Naval and Air Base in the South Pacific. Heavily defended, it was never taken over, just cut-off.

One of the messages that was sent to General Vandergrift on board ship was "unloading entirely out of hand" and that they needed the combat troops to help with the cargo. When the General came ashore at 1400 he was reluctant to order the troops to help on the beach because he still expected an enemy counter-attack. The supplies piled up and to make it worse we were four miles east of Lunga Point which was the beach area nearest the airfield. This SNAFU was thanks to the Navy putting us where they felt safer, not for the Marines.

THE BATTLES FOR GUADALCANAL

There were many individual battles fought on land, in the air and at sea starting on 8 August and lasting for the duration. All of them have been well documented in books, movies and museums. I have only personal antidotes to add to some of them from what I saw and heard first hand being there. Many of those events impacted my duties as a Quartermaster which I will try to explain.

A Japanese bomber sank one of our transport ships, the *USS George Elliott*, the first afternoon. Half of its supplies were lost. The other transports pulled out that evening expecting to return later the next day to unload their precious war cargo. All of a sudden the Navy Brass got panicked about losing more ships and not being able to defend themselves against the Japs. Perhaps they were right because that night they suffered the worst defeat in Naval history losing four cruisers in *The Battle of Savo Island*. Japanese Admirals liked to engage at night and we did not have the right tactics to defend ourselves. Radar technology was available, but too new to be used correctly, so we were literally blindsided. We woke up the next day to the sight of burning ships and hundreds of dead sailors, coated in diesel oil, floating toward the beaches.

I had the sickening feeling in my stomach that we were now considered expendable. Cut-off from getting the supplies ashore by ship, and although we had secured the airfield, it would be a long time before any planes could come to our rescue because the Japs still controlled the sky. This was the predicament that we now faced and we were totally on our own. The first four days and nights I stayed on the beach coordinating the humping of supplies up to Henderson Field and the perimeter units set up around the base. I knew food and medical supplies were especially low, at only 30 days, for an extended fight. Many of the supplies we did have had been left-overs from WWI. We did capture some supplies from the Nips, if you liked rice and dried fish for protein and bad saki.

I was somewhat surprised to learn that I had been promoted to rank of Sergeant (E-5) after just two weeks ashore. I guess that's called a damn *Battlefield Promotion?* The logistics we dealt with involved how to ration out what supplies we did have. Only two C-rations a day began to be the norm. Lives hung in the balance if fellow Marines ran out of ammo or medical supplies based on our decisions.

The Marines soon started calling this place *"Starvation Island"* and the mission renamed *"Operation Shoestring."* Once again Marines had to learn to do more with less. The other priority was finishing the all important airfield (named for Major Lofton Henderson who was killed at Midway) for our fighters and bombers. The 3,778 foot runway was almost complete when handed to us without any initial fighting. We soon learned how to utilize the abandoned Japanese construction equipment to finish the job.

Thankfully, on 20 August, squadrons of the rugged *Grumman F4F Wildcat* fighters finally began to land along with a dozen brand new *SPD Dauntless* dive bombers. We began calling them *The Cactus Air Force* after the code word for *Guadalcanal.* They were our angels arriving from the sky. They literally saved us from being killed by the bombs and strafing from the daily air-raids while on that island.

AIR RAIDS & BOMBARDMENTS

We soon began to settle into some sort of routine. General Vandergrift and his staff set up their HQ and quickly got about their business of establishing a strong defensive perimeter around the airbase. They also had Col. Edson's Raiders, being brought back from Tulagi, to defend along what came to be known as *"The Ridge."* With help from the British we enlisted native islanders and *Coast Watchers** to provide valuable intel on enemy troop positions and military

Coast Watcher Memorial on Guadalcanal, Dedicated 2011

movements. We learned early on after Colonel Goettge, our Intelligence Officer, was assassinated and his squad killed in an ambush and their bodies mutilated by those yellow son's of bitches. We were now fighting an enemy that could not be trusted and it was kill or be killed, while taking no prisoners. We adapted to that new reality very quickly. Every morning the Coast Watchers would radio the position and numbers of Jap planes headed toward us from Rabaul. Our Hellcat fighters would scramble to reach an altitude so they could intercept their bombers as air raid sirens would predictably warn us of their imminent arrival. This got to be our new normal. We could not stop work to go to a shelter all the time so we took our chances "to dance with the devil."

*Coast Watchers were volunteers as owners of plantations in the island chain. (Usually British & Australian) When war broke out they helped communicate Japanese military movements throughout the Solomons via radio and were generally assisted by brave islanders.

At night, without any Naval support, their ships would slip down "The Slot" unchallenged with what we called *The Tokyo Express* and shell us all night. We named these nights "Purple Nights." We did go to the dugout shelters because those damn 14 inch shells from their battleships would do major damage. Sleep was always at a premium and many of

Red Beach Landing Zone (LZ) at Guadalcanal

us got that dreaded "thousand mile stare" while trying to stay awake and stay alive. We just got tired of getting showered with coral rock and bomb fragments. Our Marines were seriously pissed-off by not being able to fight back at the Jap positions and especially being left alone with Navy Brass "not having our six." We felt Navy leadership sucked at that point.

After the first month on *The Canal*, things started to improve a little by mid-September. There were Marine reinforcements arriving with Chesty Puller's Seventh Marines from Samoa and some ships started to land their supplies. We even got to set up our tents and overall conditions seemed better. I sensed the pace of everything was quickening and the SeaBees started to construct a second airfield for the fighters.

We knew that the Nips were landing their own highly experienced Sendai troops on other parts of the island and there was soon going to be full frontal attacks, most likely at night. The strategy of sending wave after wave of soldiers in "Banzai Charges" to overwhelm the enemy had worked elsewhere. Guadalcanal would be different once the Marines realized they could defeat that style of warfare. All of our battles ended with massive Japanese casualties because we stood our ground and held on after wave after wave fell to our firepower. Their soldiers would drink saki before attacking and yell out across the line: "You die tonight Maallineee." Then screaming at us: "Banzai..Banzai."

Flares would first light up the sky and they would soon trip our tin-can lines and barbed wire signaling us that they were coming. Their code of fighting to the death just meant they would keep coming towards our machine guns, mortars and rifle platoons. Although I was rear echelon we were always called up to the line to provide extra rifle firepower. There was little difference of what you did on *The Canal* during the major attacks. Even cooks came forward. We all fought like hell to stay alive. At night you are shooting mostly at their silhouettes. I fired my trusty Springfield 03 at will towards any target that I saw coming at us from my foxhole. You never knew if your bullets hit any of the attackers during this chaos. With all the noise, smoke and darkness, it didn't matter in the *fog of war*. All that mattered was the Marine "to the right of you" and the Marine "to the left of you." Your goddam *Band of Brothers* were there with you and for you. Finally, hours later, we heard the orders "cease fire" and totally drenched from sweat and exhausted, we slumped back down into our muddy foxhole before counting up the night's casualties.

The Henderson Field perimeter, that the Marines fiercely defended, was only 15 square miles (roughly half the size of Ocean City, NJ) while the Japanese could land anywhere else they wanted to, and they did so with no resistance. By mid-October the enemy began a heavy build-up of troops and equipment with a two night barrage of Henderson Field, later just known as *The Bombardment*. This was done to soften up

Newspaper Headlines - October 28, 1942

our ability to counter attack by air during the landing of their five troop transports. One Marine noted that: "the enemy was landing their soldiers faster than we can kill them."

Ten days later the Japanese began the worse attack of the campaign known as *Bloody Ridge* where our lines were stretched so thin that the Japs did break through in some spots and had to be repelled. Thankfully, Army National Guard units had just arrived and helped back up the Marines.

Along with the additional manpower, the Army brought much needed supplies and armaments. Unfortunately, they were meant for their own men, not our guys. For example, they had the newer M1 Garand rifles which fired clips of bullets at a time. (Marines were always down the supply chain from Army units, that was how it worked in the War Department.) Thus began what Marine Quartermasters started calling *"midnight requisitions"* of Army supplies. Okay, I confess!

In between the major battles we started to receive the all important *Mail Call* of letters from home. About 1 October, I got the first batch of 18 letters, mostly from my parents, but also other family and friends. The first one had been mailed 25 July, so it took awhile. My first letter home was written 8 October, two months in, and we could not reveal any facts about the battle, or the censors would cut it out. We did start to find out that *Guadalcanal* was becoming a big story back in the States and my family must have realized that I was there. Dad went to the Public Library to find out exactly where it was in The South Pacific. Stories were being written about the individual heroics and the major battles; like the *Battle of the Tenaru, Edson's Ridge* and Naval defeats at *Savo Island* . Hollywood quickly joined in with the film *Guadalcanal Diary* for public consumption and support.

This publicity seemed to prompt all sorts of letter writing to our Marines. On 14 November (our 100th day on *The*

Canal), I personally received 50 letters and packages. My Mother wrote almost daily, with mostly gossip of one sort or another. She ended every letter writing: "May God bless you and take care of you. Lots of Love, Mother." One package from my Father was a new pipe which I really appreciated. Now I could go around acting like my favorite Marine, Lt. Col. Lewis "Chesty" Puller, who was always seen with his pipe.

Meanwhile the days dragged on with the constant attacks. We made the best of it and joked about such things as *Louie the Louse*, a Jap spotter plane that droned over our heads signaling for the bombings to come. Also *Washing Machine Charlie*, a single bomber, would harass us every night. I started to notice salty language was becoming the norm, and many Marines were starting to loose the discipline we had been instilled with back as a Boot. Officers still ordered us to shave and bathe daily if possible, mostly in the rivers. We were told to SITFU (Suck it the F_ up) when our dungarees tore apart from being wet all the time and we were hungry and sick. Chesty Puller started calling us "Raggedy Ass Marines" a moniker which gave us a perverse sense of pride. After all, Chesty was "The Marine's Marine" and all the enlisted men looked up to him because he told it like it was. All we had were each other, the Marine Esprit-de-Corp and leaders like, Admiral Halsey* and General Vandergrift.

* In mid-October, the Navy put Bull Halsy in charge of the Pacific Fleet and just like that morale on the Canal immediately began to

improve. His orders to us were succinct and to the point; "Kill Japs, Kill Japs, Kill More Japs".

There was always the fear that those sneaky slant-eye gooks would sneak into camp at night and kill as many Marines as possible before being killed. Some spoke English, but had trouble pronouncing words that started with the letter "L", like "latrine." So the daily password would be an 'L' word to use at night when going to the latrine or moving about when stopped by the posted sentries. Eventually the word "Lilliputian" was used and one Marine, with a terrible stutter, had such a hard time getting it out he told the sentry:

Bath Time on The Canal: Courtesy Life Magazine.

"Oh hell, just shoot me." That became the best story that week.

Before we defeated The Sendai Division during the *Battle of Bloody Ridge* 23-28 October, the feeling around camp was that we could still lose Henderson Field and if that happened we would be driven back into the sea. Chesty told his men to take to the jungle and keep fighting a "guerrilla type" war. When we emerged as victors, we felt that may have been their last stand. Marine leaders soon ordered that we surgically go on the attack as the enemy regrouped beyond our lines and we could finally show some offense while still defending the airfield. Although we were exhausted and increasingly sick from malaria it made sense to now take the battle to them. At this point, it is early November and we are into our fourth month on *The Canal*. Another large Japanese task force of 12 transports and cargo ships started coming down *The Slot* headed right for us on 11 November. We knew this would mean more shelling from their ships to protect the invasion force. We also sensed that this may be their final gamble to retake the island. However, this time our Navy was more than ready and Halsey threw everything he had at the Japs including the aircraft carrier *USS ENTERPRISE*. During the *Naval Battle of Guadalcanal*, (13-15 Nov.) we sank 28 of their ships and eliminated 10 transports from landing troops and supplies. The mighty Imperial Navy would never recover. *Skylark Channel* was soon renamed *Iron Bottom Sound* as the final resting place for over forty ships. *Game Over!* America had regained faith in itself again to win in War.

Army units arriving in late November were no longer reinforcements. They were "relieving" the victorious FMD. On 9 December (one year after declaring war on Japan) the initial Marine units began to board transports. Although the fighting would continue for another six weeks, as mostly a mopping up operation, the outcome was never again in doubt.

The final FMD toll was 650 killed and 1,278 wounded. In addition, over eight thousand suffered from malaria and other jungle diseases. Japanese losses, still have not been fully accounted for, but it was much more than the combined Allied figures. This count does not include the Navy, Army and Coast Guard losses, which when combined, numbered in the thousands.

DEPARTING THE SOLOMONS

It took several days to get all the units of our Division loaded aboard the troop ships. I was to board the *USS HUNTER-LIGGETT*, the same rust bucket of a ship that brought me to Guadalcanal. On 15 December the division set sail in a convoy for Brisbane, Australia. It would be a welcomed week's long journey to a friendly, safe place for our "Rest & Refit" (R&R) assignment. Consuming that first hot chow and Cup of Joe on ship was confirmation that we were on our way back to a civilized world, one that we had lost

4 February 1943.

Cited in the Name of

The President of the United States

THE FIRST MARINE DIVISION, REINFORCED

Staff Sergeant Wilbert F. West, U. S. M. C. R.

Under command of

Major General Alexander A. Vandegrift, U.S.M.C.

CITATION:

"The officers and enlisted men of the First Marine Division, Reinforced, on August 7 to 9, 1942, demonstrated outstanding gallantry and determination in successfully executing forced landing assaults against a number of strongly defended Japanese positions on Tulagi, Gavutu, Tanambogo, Florida and Guadalcanal, British Solomon Islands, completely routing all the enemy forces and seizing a most valuable base and airfield within the enemy zone of operations in the South Pacific Ocean. From the above period until 9 December, 1942, this Reinforced Division not only held their important strategic positions despite determined and repeated Japanese naval, air and land attacks, but by a series of offensive operations against strong enemy resistance drove the Japanese from the proximity of the airfield and inflicted great losses on them by land and air attacks. The courage and determination displayed in these operations were of an inspiring order."

Secretary of the Navy.

Presidential Citation to Staff Sergeant W. F. West

47

touch with for the past five months. Next on board ship, we all patiently awaited our turn for a scaldingly hot shower to wash the stink of the jungle off of our bodies. It would be a much longer time before we could lose the stench inside our nostrils of all of those dead decaying bodies. Getting rid of the malarial parasites and other jungle diseases, which caused Marines to burn-up with fevers, would also take time and much needed medical help. Every Marine left a part of themselves on *The Canal*. Myself included.

I was one of the many that had come down with Malaria and Dengue Fever. The Officers and Enlisted Men alike shared these maladies. The Navy Corpsmen on board ship administered a newly developed synthetic substitute for Quinine, a malarial drug named "Atabrine." That would have to hold us until we made it to a field hospital somewhere in Australia. On average we had lost over twenty-five pounds each and the signs of "combat fatigue" were etched in our faces. We no longer wanted to just go to that next island and "kill more Japs." Although we did not fear our enemy, we just wanted rest and recuperation from the jungle.

Chapter 5

From Hell to Heaven in Melbourne

As we sailed *south by southwest* towards the continent of Australia we still worried that Japanese submarines or even spotter aircraft could find us out at sea. At night strict orders were given: "No lights will be shown on the weather decks." That also meant: "the smoking lamp was out."

Army Four Star General Douglas MacArthur had established his South Pacific Command in Brisbane, in the State of Queensland, after he retreated from the Philippines. "Dugout Doug" had earned that unflattering nickname when he hid out in the Malinta Tunnel in Corregidor while his troops were being shelled just before he fled the islands leaving thousands to suffer and die during the *Battan Death March*. MacArthur gave the order for the FMD to do their R&R in Queensland, alongside his own Army command, as they prepared for what was to come next. The problem we faced was that this part of the world was still very tropical and was hardly the place we needed to recover from tropical diseases. Many of our men were saying; "Hell if this is the best they can do, why not just leave us on Guadalcanal." General Vandergrift agreed and intervened to send us much further south to Melbourne, Victoria where the climate was cooler and there were fewer mosquitos. The problem now was how to get us down there with no readily available ships.

When Admiral Halsey heard of our plight, he abruptly ordered Navy transports to Brisbane, primarily the *USS WEST POINT,* which had been the ocean liner *SS AMERICA.* Before we could be properly rescued from Old Dugout Doug, we did get to spend Christmas in Brisbane, with very little celebration, just thankful for the "glad tidings" of being alive which was enough for most of us war weary souls. The Red Cross had arranged for holiday packages and we received Coca-Cola to have with our Christmas Dinner. A week later, for New Year's Eve 1943, we got a double ration of warm beer.

Another SNAFU occurred getting us ferried onto the *USS West Point.* It so happened that the channel to the Port was not deep enough for the draft of an ocean liner. Barges were needed to ferry us to the ship which was anchored 17 miles offshore. We finally left Brisbane on 10 January 1943 and arrived in Melbourne two days later to a surprise *Hero's Welcome.* As soon as we disembarked, Melbourne became the very civilized place we had prayed and wanted it to be. We were called *"The Saviors of Australia"* in the local newspapers. The overwhelming reception we received led to an almost immediate interaction and connection with all Australian citizenry. The phrase "my house is your house" was never more true as it was now "down under."

Strangers took us in as if we were long lost family. The basic daily greeting was: "Good on Ya Yank" or "Hello Mate" as they announced it enthusiastically in their local accent.

After we landed to the cheering locals at Port Melbourne, we were put on trains or trucks to our new camps. The whole division could not all bivouac in one place, so we were split up at various locations around the city and suburbs. Some were in outdoor sporting arenas like the Melbourne Cricket Grounds. Other were assigned to Australian Military Bases. FMD's Headquarters Battalion, which I was part of, was sent to Camp Balcombe. This was located in Mount Martha down the peninsula south of Melbourne along the coast. Our camp consisted of rows of green eight-man pyramid tents and a few permanent buildings including a field hospital and a PX. January in the Southern Hemisphere is their summer time, but it was also in the cooler State of Victoria. Therefore, we now had a much better climate to recover from our tropical diseases. As I got to know our new environs I was struck by how much it reminded me of home. The size of this city was much like Philadelphia. They had trams, we had trolleys. They had lots of gardens and parks along St. Kilda Road, we had beautiful Fairmount Park. But most of all they had many lonely single young women* and they were not shy about approaching us for a conversation and possibly a date.

*Many Aussie men at that time were already assigned overseas.

We had accrued many months of back pay due us to spend on liberty around town. When those funds ran out there were many card games and the selling of war souvenirs to make a few bucks. We were given free rides on public transportation and "comped" in many bars and restaurants. Back at the camp PX, I bought pipe tobacco and of all things, cold milk. You have no idea how refreshing that glass of cold milk tasted the first few times. During the early weeks in camp there was little structure and we would take liberty freely. Unfortunately, we were based about 30 miles from downtown Melbourne. A couple of my tent-mates, not too weak from malaria, decided to venture into town on our first weekend. The three of us had heard of a popular pub, *The Young & Jackson Hotel,* directly across from the train station. When we arrived it was packed with fellow Marines all having a good time and letting off steam. Once inside we ordered some pints of Fosters, a popular Melbourne beer. After quenching our thirst with a few Fosters we decided to look around the hotel and stumbled upon '*Chloe*', the life-sized nude portrait of a young French girl. She became a popular site for our horny Marines. Next we wanted some good old fish & chips and found the perfect place nearby. It was run by a nice family whose three daughters waitressed there and they became the first girls our age we interacted with since leaving the States. After our meal, we were introduced to the daughters by their mother and it almost felt like being home.

MALARIA TREATMENTS

Due to the sheer number of Marines with malaria, our field hospital could only handle so many cases each week. The fellas with the very worst cases were shipped stateside. Depending on the severity of each man's condition, we were given a rotating schedule to follow and when to come to the hospital for treatment. You never really get malaria out of your blood stream once you have it. We had strict orders to keep taking our Atabrine. The sweats and alternating chills from malaria would disable you from doing anything and often you just wanted to curl up in your bunk and feel like dying. I also got severe headaches with my attacks. However, over the next several months I slowly started to feel better and put weight back on as my strength returned. When not in the hospital I returned to my Quartermaster's work at Battalion HQ and began doing physical exercises and marches around the camp. We were soon given uniforms with the newly created shoulder patch for the FMD with the Guadalcanal designation over *The Southern Cross* stars.

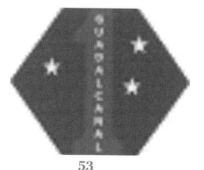

"ME" Photo sent to parents in July 1943 to show that I was ok and had regained weight. Outside my pyramid tent - Camp Balcombe.

On Washington's Birthday, 22 February 1943, the entire division assembled to *Parade March* through downtown Melbourne as a big "Thank You" to our host city. For over six miles we were cheered by the entire populace that had come out to see their heroes and hear the Marine Band play such standards as "Semper Fidelis," "The Marine Hymn" *and* "The Star-Spangled Banner."

Someone in the crowd mumbled; "Just look at Uncle Sam's Marines showing off for our Sheilas."*

*Sheila is an Australian slang word for girls.

Following behind our group was an Australian Military Band that played their own popular march, "Waltzing Matilda." This particular march resonated with a lot of us and appealed to our need for a home away from home. So much so, that it was eventually adopted as the FMD's official march, and is still played today. I especially liked it since it was Mother's name, although everyone at home called her Tillie.

MEETING A VERY PRETTY NURSE

After my first couple of hospital visits I noticed a pretty nurse assigned to my ward. She seemed to stand out from the others in my personal opinion. One morning this nurse came over to my bed and said she would be taking care of me that day. She politely introduced herself as Nurse Jean. I replied by telling her that I liked to be called Bill, not Wilbert.

She took my vitals right away and saw that I still had a fever from the malaria. She also had a checklist of questions to complete for my medical records and efficiently went through them as she probably had done hundreds of times already. I answered each question and tried to make eye contact in between, but she kept her head down looking at her clipboard. When she finished her task and was sure I had been taking my medications and everything was ok for now, she asked me a little about myself. Where was I from? How long I had been in the Marines? I wished that this was a sign that she was interested in me personally, but knew that it was probably just her way of getting comfortable with a new patient. I really hoped she would continue caring for me during my hospital stays and built up enough courage to request it directly. To which she shyly replied: "Well Bill, I would like that too." I felt my heart rate jump right then.

Sure enough, as fate would have it, Nurse Jean began taking care of me during my next regular hospital stays. Over the next few weeks we began sharing a lot more details of our personal history and stories about family and home life. I dropped hints that I would like to know more about her family and even seeing her outside of the hospital. Initially she resisted my advances because she must have felt it was unprofessional. I knew there were other nurses that had started seeing some of their Marine patients and the Doctors were not going to interfere as long as it was consensual.

Eventually Jean invited for me to come over to her family's house for Easter Sunday dinner which was on 25 April 1943. The invitation included staying overnight so it would not require me getting back late at night to Camp Balcombe. The whole day was enjoyable and reminded me of two long years ago when I last had any holiday gatherings with my family. After that Easter Sunday together, Jean and I started seeing each other on a regular basis whenever we could. Having a steady girlfriend, that was also my nurse, made my recovery that much faster and easier to endure.

Soon after Easter the weather in Melbourne started changing to colder and rainier days. It was already their Autumnal season and would soon be going into winter.

Other changes were happening as well. The FMD had a new General in charge, Major General Rupertus. Several Marines were awarded the Medal of Honor for their heroics on *The Canal*. We were officially issued the M1 Garand rifle and we began to intensify training drills for those who were physically able. We knew at some point we would most likely be headed back to combat and we had to be ready. Our camp was just off the coastline and was used to practice landing drills we called: "Mount Martha Maneuvers."

Australian soldiers were starting to filter back from the North African campaign. We called them *Diggers* which went back to a WWI reference and was considered an unflattering nickname. Many of the *Diggers* resented our presence around town and were also jealous of the Marines that had been dating their girls. Quite often fist-fights would break-out in pubs or even on the street with our fellas having to defend themselves. We had combined social/sporting events, during our days in Melbourne, which certainly provided the opportunity for the two nations to try and show who was better in these not so friendly competitions. Then there was a highly anticipated *Beer Social*, specifically ordered without any Military Police presence, and enthusiastically attended by some 9,000 thirsty soldiers, half of them Aussies. It would go on to forge an unbreakable bond between us and just like that the fights stopped. I got to enjoy Aussie Rules Football which was close to our football except you kicked the ball forward instead of passing it. I have to admit those *Aussie Blokes* were a tough breed and very much equal to our Marines. They were a fun bunch to have a beer with once you got to know them and their sense of humor.

Jean was also fun to be with and we enjoyed seeing some of the sights around Melbourne together. In the winter months we often went to the movies or to hear live music at one of the bandstands. We even danced to Glenn Miller's Big Band music, which was popular back then, and very much my favorite. There was always, in the background, the knowledge that eventually I would be shipping out and we would be separated by an ocean as the war waged on. We accepted that fact and just wanted to enjoy the times that we did have together. We also held out hope that after the next deployment was over the Marines would somehow get to return to Melbourne.

Being a Quartermaster I usually got early word of plans when the FMD would get orders to move out. By mid-August we began sending Engineers and Sea-Bees to the south-eastern coast of New Guinea to set up forward base camps in territory controlled by the Allies. That told me that by end of September most of the rest of us would have to follow. There were many Marines that had fallen in love, like I had, and proposed to their sweethearts before they shipped out. Quite a few even took the plunge and had gotten married before leaving. Searching my heart for the proper thing to do, I decided to ask Jean to marry me before I left her alone in Australia. I did not know if I would ever come back alive or even ever return to Melbourne, but to me it was what I needed to do, especially given the circumstances we were facing. I scrambled to come up with the cash to buy a decent engagement ring. On 23 September, two days before I was to ship out, I visited Jean's parents and asked them permission to marry their only daughter. They agreed and then I turned on one knee to Jean and proposed. She accepted and I slipped the ring onto her trembling finger. We spent our last night together at her parent's home. When would I get to see Jean again? What fate would this crazy war hold for us?

Chapter 6

Operation Cartwheel: Isolate Rabaul

After nine months in Melbourne I reluctantly boarded a Victory Ship named the *USS GEORGE S. BOUTWELL* on 25 September 1943. We did not get to sail on the newer Navy APA assault transports, set up for Marine deployments like this, but instead on this ship designed for cargo not troops. Again we improvised, adapted and overcame by building heads, showers and galleys on the weather deck. The Army Brass again had "stuffed us"* Marines. Early the next day we sailed away from Port Melbourne to a royal sendoff while the bands played "Waltzing Matilda." I spotted Jean standing on the dock with tears in her eyes as we shoved off. We blew some final kisses to one another. Several Marines inflated condoms and dropped them over the side as their farewell.

*An Australian expression for 'F-U' that we adopted.

As our convoy sailed northward hugging the eastern coast of Australia I realized what a beautiful country I was leaving behind and to have been here for so long was something to be extremely grateful for. I also thought that I had to get back here again so I could finally reconnect with the woman I loved and decide to get married.

General MacArthur's strategy was to island hop to fulfill his promise of "I Shall Return" to the Philippines by first going through New Guinea. He did not want to take on the Japanese Naval base at Rabaul directly because of their strong defenses, but rather isolate and bomb it with our long distance B-17's. However, on his flank was a smaller Japanese airbase at Cape Gloucester (just west of Rabaul) in the New Britain Island chain that had to be eliminated. General MacArthur would use his *Sixth Army* along with the *FMD* as the amphibious assault force to accomplish this mission.

Our convoy first stopped at a tiny nowhere place called Townsville, Queensland for a brief overnight resupply on 4 October before sailing the next morning for Goodenough Island in New Guinea. We finally arrived on 9 October, after traveling over two thousand nautical miles. The FMD would be scattered along the coast at three forward bases. Each of these bases were also used by the Doggies who were, as usual, better supplied than we were. Once again our Marines made a confiscatory practice of foraging off of these Army supplies as part sport and part survival. As Quartermaster, I appreciated anything they acquired which would help "the cause."

Our HQ base was 50 miles off the eastern tip of New Guinea. The Aussies had recently recaptured the island's airfield from the Japanese and it was an important staging area for this campaign. At this point in the war, men and material were arriving from the States in greater quantities and providing logistical support was paramount in this battle.

In late November I got to see firsthand our so called leader General MacArthur, with his "silly ass" Corncob pipe, as he arrived by plane on Goodenough Island to inspect the troops and plan the Cape Gloucester landings.

New Guinea was still just another tropical shit-hole with heat, humidity, snakes and all sorts of bugs. However, we were so much better equipped to deal with it. We had Quonset huts with electricity to work and sleep in. As part of HQ Battalion we had decent chow and hot showers. We were also getting mail and care packages on a regular basis. As a matter of fact, it turned out that more mail was flowing to and from Melbourne than from The States. I even had a manual typewriter to prepare my supply requisition paperwork. I guess Goodenough Island would have to be "good enough" for however long I was going to be there. At least there were no bombs falling on us daily, and we got to sleep above ground.

By the end of October all of the FMD had finally shipped out of Melbourne and were in our newly constructed bases. Plans were well underway for the next assault and it seemed to be happening right around Christmas. Our attack forces were combat loaded 24 December aboard the *LST's*. On the day after Christmas 1943, the *Old Breed* went ashore again in the South Pacific and again were unopposed, this time landing at Cape Gloucester. I was not personally part of these landing as I stayed back on Goodenough Island supporting the supply efforts. Just as important for me personally, I was studying for an exam for promotion to 'E5' Staff Sergeant.

This would be my second Christmas away from home and perhaps the most emotional given my separation from Jean and feeling extremely homesick. I did receive fifteen letters from family and friends and three from Jean right before Christmas. I liked keeping score of when these letters were written and when I finally got to read them. The movie they showed that Christmas Eve was *The Gay Sisters* with Barbara Stanwyck and George Brent. For Christmas dinner we had Turkey with all the fixings. This was a big improvement over last year when we were just lucky to have left *The Canal* alive. Some Marines got sloppy drunk on extracting *Aqua-Velva* and other alcoholic ingredients they found around base. I wrote a long letter to my family updating them on my better conditions and describing what I

Sergeant Bill West on Goodenough Island

though might be happening back home around the Christmas Tree based on memories of earlier years on Blavis Street. I felt that if I could envision everyone's part in these solemn traditions it would be as if I was there with them. I needed those visions this Christmas, above all others, and promised to myself that I would always respect and celebrate the importance of the birth of the Baby Jesus. The three letters I received from Jean were updates on her delicate condition and plans for the New Year back in Melbourne. I decided it was time for me to tell someone back home about my engagement and what that meant personally. I could not tell my parents as they would worry too much. So I would secretly write to my sister Mildred and mail it to her office building at Provident Trust in Philadelphia. Between 19 January and 29 February, I wrote three times detailing to her the situation I faced and asking for her advice. Each letter was followed by a reply with words of wisdom only an older sister could evoke.

CAPE GLOUCESTER CAMPAIGN

The Marines dubbed the jungles at Cape Gloucester: "*The Green Inferno.*" As a tropical rainforest it was the wettest place on earth during the monsoon season. All of our vehicles got bogged down and marching through the swamps was exhausting. Just like on *The Canal* our troops were wet all the time and these conditions again took a physical and psychological toll. Many Marines, about fifty, were killed or injured by rotted falling trees during the battle. Despite these conditions, First Marines were once again able to scatter those f'in little Nip bastards inland and capture with little resistance their airfield by 30 December 1943.

On 20 March 1944, I boarded the Royal Naval ship, *MS ANHUI,* and arrived at our forward staging base, Oro Bay in Papua, New Guinea the next day. Our orders were to proceed directly for Cape Gloucester almost three months after the initial assault. Essentially we were part of a *mop-up operation* at the tail end of this campaign. As a QM-SGT, I saw why we had been constantly reissuing clothing and equipment due to the rotting and mold from the climate here. Everything not covered or protected would rot out. My pipe tobacco if smoked would make me sick after being waterlogged. My pictures of Jean and all my letters did get special care and were safely wrapped in rubber. By the time we arrived, the engineers had built some huts for us to stay in so thankfully we did not have to use the new jungle hammocks that the infantry had been issued. We all hoped that the sooner we got this over with we would be sent back to Melbourne. After my month on *The Cape,* the fighting had mostly ceased and the FMD was being relieved from their combat role. On 29 April 1944 we loaded onto the *USS Libra,* an attack cargo ship. Marine General Rupertus was supposed to have said that we were going back to Melbourne. That would not be the case.

Chapter 7

Pavuvu Island: "The Death of Hope"

It sounds like a joke right? It was **no** joke and actually
the joke was on us thinking we would once again get to
experience Melbourne. Pavuvu was a singular island in the
Russell Island Chain about 65 miles west of Guadalcanal.
Based on just a onetime flyover our brilliant officers saw nice
sandy beaches and neat rows of palm trees and decided to
base our Division there until the next campaign. We
disembarked on 3 May 1944 and set up our "rest camp" in an
area of palms that had been cleared away just days before. I
was distraught now knowing that I would not be seeing my
fiancé anytime soon. I even sought solace from the Division
Chaplain. He told me to pray and how God can work in
strange ways. This certainly was a strange way in my mind.
However, scuttlebutt was that this island would also be where
replacement Marines would be coming in to complete their
training. This gave me some hope that I may be rotated back
to The States. I still had work to do on Pavuvu in getting the
camp set up and properly supplied. Ships from forward bases
like Guadalcanal could now supply us within a day or two. We
had six to eight men in a tent and it was still rainy season so
mud was everywhere again. Added to our frustrations were
rats scurrying around at night and large land crabs invading
the tents looking for shelter in our damn boots.

GOING "ASIATIC"

After all we went through the past two years and especially with the conditions living in these jungles many of the men developed a psychological condition that we called "Asiatic." This was a reference to spending too much time in this part of the world. An eccentric and crazed pattern of behavior which could and did ultimately end in self harm and or suicide. Worse yet, fellow Marines hardly seemed to notice when someone went bonkers. Had we reached the point that we were beyond caring? Some of the worst cases saw men shipped to another island named Banika which was set up as a Naval field hospital. The ones deemed as potentially suicidal were put in cages, like jail cells, so they could do no harm as they were being medicated. It almost became like a *Catch 22*. You probably were a little crazy just by living through these campaigns. Being in the rear-echelon as a QM was no cake walk but nothing like what the front line Marines experienced. My own sanity was also being impacted by imagining what was going on back in Australia. After a couple of weeks on Pavuvu we began to get mail again. I had also written Jean a couple of times to inform her about our status. She had written me every week with updates and the back of each envelope had the large letters S.W.A.K. (Sealed with a Kiss) in bright red lipstick.

ROTATION OUT OF THE COMBAT ZONE

During the past two and a half years, ever since the war began, the Marines had built up a sizable fighting force with thousands of new recruits. By June 1944, many of these had started to arrive at Pavuvu as FMD replacements. Marine Corps policy was that after 24 months in a combat zone, and 'IF' a replacement was available, you would be put on a list to rotate out. We had heard that Marine Brass had travelled to *The Pentagon* just to make sure that the eligible men would get to go home. There were 260 Officers and 4,600 enlisted men who became eligible for a lottery process that required you had also displayed a good service record and maintained satisfactory ratings from your commanding officers. I did win this lottery and was informed I would be going stateside.

I was given a pamphlet entitled *A Marine's Short Course on Personal Manners During Rotation*. Basically it advised us on how to re-adjust to being back in the USA. It was done somewhat tongue-in-cheek but was a tangible sign that I was exiting this hell hole. It mentioned things not to say as; "throw down the grease" but instead say; "please pass the butter." I was asked by many of the fellas that I had gotten to know, that could not leave, if I would take down their family's name and address to call or telegram their loved ones when I got back to the States. Just to let them know that they were still 'OK.' We did know firsthand that there would still be many island invasions to go until Tojo was finally defeated.

Chapter 8

New Duty Roster: Going Stateside

My orders came down that I would be leaving Pavuvu on 24 June 1944 bound for San Diego, California aboard the *USS GENERAL JOHN POPE,* a troop transport. This was none too soon after seven long weeks just surviving the horrendous conditions on Pavuvu. Once I arrived at the Marine Base in San Diego I would receive further orders. A few last minute details required that we turn in our '782' gear, mess kits, ponchos, and the like for reuse. We were further reminded once stateside; "that we should still behave as gentlemen even if we were coming back from the South Seas."

When it came time to board our transport in Masquitti Bay nearly all the fellas came down to the pier to see us off. It was hard to say goodbye to those not leaving. We were happy to go but certainly not gloating over our own good fortune. As we marched onto the ship the Division Band played "Maizy Doats" and "California Here We Come." When we shoved off I heard the Band begin to play the "Marine Hymn" and instantly those deep emotions suddenly unmasked a stream of tears. I began to sob uncontrollably. And as I looked around, I was not alone. All I could think was; "West you made it out alive and my Mother's prayers had been answered." I was one of the lucky ones today, but my inner thoughts went back to Melbourne as we headed further away from where I felt I needed to be. Back with Jean in Australia.

For the next two weeks we would set a steady course to the north and east without much fear of Japanese Naval interference which had been greatly reduced the past two years. As luck would have it, we re-crossed the Equator on 1 July, exactly two years to the day after my initiation with King Neptune. A non-event this time as we were more than qualified to have passed this ancient ceremony. The Navy had learned a lot in two years about how to properly transport troops. We were actually the first Marines to return stateside under what I would call: "normal circumstances." We were not being evacuated due to injury, or other medical reasons. We also did not have special orders for those needed back at Marine Bases for debriefing or training. We had honestly earned our way back home under Marine Corps protocol.

Our ship pulled into San Diego's Naval Base on the morning of 7 July 1944. This was our "Independence Day" only three days later. It was a warm, typically sunny California day, but with no tropical humidity, which to all of us returning Marines almost seemed too good to be true. There had to be a catch, but there was none this time. There was certainly no fanfare for us on this arrival. The Navy Yard was bustling with the job at hand and busy supporting the ongoing war effort throughout the Pacific Theater.

For the next week we would stay at the Marine Base in San Diego awaiting orders. We would have this time to climatize being back stateside, almost like a quarantine. We were checked out by Doctors and made sure we were not bringing back any disease that could be spread to the public. They also made sure we took our Atabrine. I did write a letter to Jean telling her I had made it back to American soil and would let her know where I would be headed next. As soon as I could, I phoned my parents letting them know the good news of my safe return home. I would call them again when I knew where I would be headed. Some of the lucky ones from our group of returnees got liberty up to Los Angeles by train for a couple of days. I stayed back, after all I was engaged.

Troop Train Headed Back East

On 13 July I got my orders (#7-44) that I was to transfer to the Marine Barracks at The Boston Navy Yard. I was to take a troop train to New York leaving 1800 hours on 14 July 1944. A trip that would travel 3,056 miles and with travel rations for only 12 meals. I would be among 65 other Marines assigned to the Boston Navy Yard and most all of us were from the East Coast. We did not have to report to duty until 19 August 1944, so we had a month's furlough to get back. I took that as a good sign that our Officers wanted us to be able to readjust with our families as much as possible until we had to go back to active duty given the length of time away.

The train initially headed north towards San Francisco and then due east stopping at large and small towns along the way. This time our train was met at almost every stop by a *Railroad Canteen* run by The Red Cross and other caring volunteers handing out free food and cigarettes. Seeing all this hometown pride gave me added appreciation for why we had been willing to fight for our way of life and how beautiful and vast this country really was. This troop transport train, specially built as a *mobile barracks,* was cramped with bunks stacked three high but we didn't mind. Given these past two years, we were living large. We passed the time playing cards and telling stories about each of our home towns. Often it would end up reliving our experiences with some teenage girlfriend and was usually exaggerated. Re-adjusting was going to take time because you just don't block out those many months in the blink of an eye. Some fellas already were having nightmares and would jump at any loud noise. Along the way we started talking about what we would do when we arrived at New York City. Should we just go home right away before reporting for duty? Or do something together in New York City? After ten long days and nights crossing the country we finally arrived at Grand Central Terminal on 24 July 1944.

Most of our guys opted to stay in NYC for a couple of days. We had been told that; "the place to go" was *The Stage Door Canteen* on 44th Street in the Theater District. It was literally in the basement of a Broadway Theater and you entered through the stage door. They were part of an Actor's service organization and would take care of any serviceman in uniform with food, coffee and entertainment all free of charge, but no booze. In addition a young, attractive hostess would share their time with you while at the *Canteen*. The only catch was that you were not to go out with any of the hostesses outside the premises. There were thirteen fellow Marines on our train that would all be going home to Philadelphia after our liberty in NYC. As a group, we decided to stick together and go to *The Stage Door*. We were treated grand as soon as we arrived. We couldn't believe how nice everyone was to us and there were five hostesses assigned to just our Philly entourage. The other thing that stood out was the "top notch" entertainers performing there. There were big-bands like Count Basie and Benny Goodman, comedians like Red Skelton and Danny Kaye and even famous actresses from Hollywood to serve as some of the hostesses. Most of the interaction with our hostesses was just small talk and we really couldn't tell them much about our last two years in the jungle. It was non-relatable to the average person. We did get to talk to some Army (Doggies) Privates who were about to ship out to England. They had never seen combat and some asked us what it was like. Again, it was just hard to relate back to them. At one point the Master of Ceremonies singled out our group and had the band play "The Marine Hymn" in our honor. Everyone in the place stood up and applauded us

Pack of playing cards given to servicemen.

when they were told we were from The First Marine Division and had just returned from overseas. I will never forget the sensation of goosebumps and how patriotic I felt at that very moment.

After two days in New York it was time to get over to Pennsylvania Station and take the train southbound for two hours to Philadelphia. I had called my sister and arranged to have her meet me at the North Philadelphia Station. I did not want my parents to meet the train because it would be too emotional I thought. I was much thinner and more weathered now, for them to see me coming off onto the train platform, from when I left 25 months earlier.

Back on Blavis Street in Philadelphia

The train arrived around noon on 26 July 1944. I had been gone for over two years and did not know how I would react to being back. Would I be a different type of son or brother than before the experiences of war? What kinds of emotions would I feel? How will I explain what happened in Melbourne, if at all? Those thoughts raced around in my head. I did have almost three weeks of the furlough left before going to Boston so it should be enough time to answer some of these questions. Mildred was on the platform as I got off the train and greeted me with a big hug and a kiss. She looked swell and no different from the last time I saw her. She had brought the family car, there were still gas rations, but we were only a few miles from home. She told me that my parents had been worried sick about what I had endured and also now that Walt was in the Army too, but not yet assigned overseas. The old neighborhood looked exactly the same as when I had left it. There were many homes with Service Star Banners* in the windows. We had a "Two Star" banner, but thankfully none in Gold, which indicating deceased.

*Service banners identified families with a son(s) serving in the war.

As we pulled up, Mother came running out to greet us with Forrest following behind. I could tell right away they had aged greatly from all the worry. My Dad, Forrest West worked in Graphic Arts as a lithographer but also managed the company's finances and production operations and never allowed himself to take a vacation. After coming into the house I went upstairs to my old room. Mother had all the letters I had written laid out as well as many articles from the local newspapers. Some of the articles were about the Marines, but many were also about Penn's football team and *The Eagles*. One was a recent article from *The Inquirer* about the 13 of us, listed by name, as the first Philadelphia area Marines to return home. After getting caught up on family matters and when dinner was over, I excused myself for the night. I had not slept much the past few days and was dead tired. I finally felt safe sleeping in my own bed again.

The next day my Father had arranged that I get fitted for a new Marine uniform at Sanders Military Uniform shop on S. 15th Street. He wanted his son to look like a proud Marine in a brand spanking new uniform which would display the Guadalcanal shoulder patch. He paid $71.15 for it which was a month's pay for me. It would be ready in a few short days so he could get pictures while I was still on furlough. It turned out that two of my cousins were also home and we arranged that Wendell Dietz who was in the 4th Marine Division and Bill Knox who was in the Navy would stopover for a group picture in our respective uniforms. Wendell would go on to fight at the Battle for Iwo Jima in February - March, 1945 and Bill served aboard a combat ship in the Pacific Theater. Both of my cousins made it back home safely after the war.

Cousins: Wendell Dietz, Bill Knox & Bill West

My orders were to report to the Marine Barracks in Charlestown, Massachusetts at 0725 on 19 August 1944. I would just miss seeing my football teams play again at Franklin Field, when the season started in September. I had a lot of things to do before leaving town. I wrote several letters to Jean in Melbourne keeping her up-to-date. I would not get her letters until I got to Boston. I also looked into what it would take with the government to bring Jean to the States as a "war bride" when the war finally ended.

My sister and I did manage to go down to our favorite shore town, Ocean City New Jersey, for a couple of days in early August and escape the city heat.

Chapter 9

Boston Marine Barracks: Good Duty

This barracks was the first one in the country, built in 1810. It was attached to The Boston Navy Yard in Charlestown, Mass. There were several original Navy Yards along the East Coast including Brooklyn, NY, Portsmouth, ME and Philadelphia, PA. During most of WWII, the Boston Navy Yard was in full production mode turning out new warships and repairing/refitting others. At its' peak it employed over 50,000 workers and was New England's single largest employer. Today, it is part of the National Parks.

After finding my way around the huge Navy Yard, I reported as ordered at Building # 1 to The Duty Officer. After completing some paperwork and a brief orientation with a few other newly assigned Marines I was shown to my bunk to drop off my sea bag and told to report to the NCO in the Quartermaster's Office downstairs at 1100 hours. I found out that there were several dozen Marines from my rotation that had been assigned here in various capacities. When word got around that there were Guadalcanal veterans in The Barracks, I had just wanted to be ignored, now I was going to be asked all kinds of things from the younger Marine and Navy enlistees. What I wanted most of all was to see if mail had yet to catch up with me from the Fleet Post Office in San Francisco. Especially any letters from Melbourne.

Adjusting to a Different Marine Life

However we tried, the Marines that had just returned from war, could not easily adjust mentally or even physically to being Stateside. It would be a slow decompression as is like coming to the surface from deep below the sea. There was the feeling of "survivor's guilt" associated with being safely home and leaving so many fellas we knew back on Pavuvu. While not knowing what was in store for them next. I also did not like being called a *hero* stateside. The heroes were the guys who never made it back. I was just one of the fortunate ones!

I learned that as a QM Staff Sergeant I would be responsible for helping all the Marines with their logistics of movement and gear based on their duty orders. My Captain was a Lawrence Denmire and there were 11 others in the QM's office. The *US War Machine* in mid-1944 was in full swing and so much had changed since we left New River 26 months ago. I had my pick of new gear and clothing. I got a brand new foot locker to fill up and the latest in work uniforms which included warmer clothes for the New England winter ahead. I had my own desk in the QM's office and was eventually promoted to *Supply Sergeant* which meant a little better pay each month.

That familiar Marine routine of discipline and professionalism began again for me at these barracks. Each morning there would be reveille at 0600. We would assemble on the parade deck directly in front of the barracks for roll-call and the day's orders and announcements. From there we would march over to the mess hall for breakfast. These meals were with real eggs, which we rarely had in the last two years, and really good hot *Joe*. My favorite breakfast was their *SOS*. (Dried beef on toast which we all called "Shit on a Shingle"). And it actually tasted like I remembered it back at New River, not watered down swill from jungle rain. After breakfast came an hour or so of physical training and then a "Triple S: shit, shave and shower." After that I reported in full uniform by 0900 to my desk in the QM office for the day's work. Each night we had to be in our bunks when taps sounded at 2200 hours. No shenanigans at this place. Since we were close to Boston's North End, which was an Italian restaurant area, some of the guys would try to make it there and back for their delicious *Cannolis* before taps were sounded.

The Marines also provided security for the Navy Base. There were still real threats of German spies and the potential for sabotage of the many valuable military assets to protect. On 26 August, just one week after getting settled into the barracks, I received orders to be an armed guard on a military truck headed to Maine. Specifically, I was "to prevent any interference with the contents of the truck, which were of a confidential nature." The truck was going to the *Bath Iron Works* Shipbuilding Yard in Bath, Maine which was 140 miles north of Boston. I literally ran "shot-gun" in the front seat of our Dodge half-ton utility truck.

It felt good that I was chosen for that type of mission and I asked to be selected again when needed for that kind of duty. Otherwise, the days were spent at a desk mostly pushing paper and organizing supplies and equipment.

Proudly displaying the Colors in Boston, 1945.

Heart Breaking News

Two weeks after arriving in Boston my backlog of mail finally caught up with me. Much of the mail addressed to the San Francisco P.O. from family and friends had stopped when it became known that I was returning to the States, but Jean was still writing to me through the military address I had given her. In the rubber-banded bundle were three hand written letters and one separate small package mailed from Australia. As soon as I saw the package my heart sank. I knew what was in it, the one thing it could only be. Jean was returning our engagement ring. Her letters explained in a progression of logical facts and jumbled emotions why she could not go through with the marriage. She felt I could never find a way to work out getting back to Melbourne, now that I was finally safely back home. Furthermore, she felt she could not risk her whole future and never seeing her family again by moving to the States. Plus, where would the money come from to afford these arrangements. It was time to move on with our lives and that was the bottom line. I felt shattered since I had made the marriage commitment to her, but she held the upper hand. I could not force her to be a *war bride*.

Other bad news followed. Word got back to us that the FMD had begun a new amphibious assault on a Japanese held island called Peleliu. D-day was 15 September and it was supposed to be just a two to three day operation according to the Generals. This was the idiot "Dug-out Doug" (MacArthur) ordering Marines to knock out a minor island airbase, miles and miles away on his flank, so he would return gallantly to the Philippines regardless of the price. This time the Japanese Army had learned their lesson and dug in on the hills above the airbase and made sure we would pay a heavy price in blood in getting them out. I knew I would have been a part of this insanity had I not fortunately rotated out when I did.

Friendly with a Navy Wave

Most Saturday nights a couple of my FMD friends and I would hang out at the enlisted men's social hall on base for a beer or two. This was available for all eligible servicemen at the Yard. It was a very relaxed atmosphere, but you had to be in uniform to gain admittance. In late October, in keeping with the Halloween Spirit, several of the *Navy Waves** which were in a support role at this Navy Base, surprised us by dressing up as male Sailors in their basic all white uniforms and crashing our social club. It was a new deal to have women in the Navy and not all the fellas took to it right away. But this night seemed different so we invited some of them to join us for a beer, regulations be damned. As it turned out I recognized one of the *Waves* from the clerical pool that had been assigned to The Quartermaster's Department.

*Navy Waves was a "Women's Reserve Branch' for both enlisted and officer service, established in 1942 for the duration of the war. The purpose was to free up men for sea duty after they were fully trained.

Her name was Helen Kennedy and she was from Cleveland, Ohio. She was not one of the Boston Kennedy's for sure, but she was Irish Catholic and still had a bit of an Irish brogue. She seemed nice but I was still *gun-shy* to get involved with anyone until this war was finally over. Also with my family, at the time, it was not acceptable to marry into the Catholic faith. We agreed to be sociable as friends and maybe share a meal together outside the base. This we did on a fairly regular basis on Sundays when we were both off-duty. It was also a good way to explore the City of Boston and its' history.

Fall of 1944 - Life Returning to Normal

Being stationed in Boston was not all that bad given the circumstances. In late September my younger brother Walt visited me on a weekend pass. He was in the Army Air Corp and was training in their weather service and took the train up from Providence. He was also taking courses at Brown University. I got to attend Harvard, but only for watching their home football games. In early October I went to see them play Boston College. I sure did miss attending college football games when I was overseas. Later in October I got a three day pass and went home to Philadelphia for Mother's 55th Birthday. It was a complete surprise to her and my Dad helped with the arrangements of my visit as well as keeping it a secret. Part of the weekend's plan was that Dad got tickets for us to go see Penn's football team play Princeton on

Saturday 21 October at Franklin Field. The next morning I caught the train back to Boston. It had been a special family reunion which probably wouldn't happen again until at least Christmas. I did like traveling around on *The Pennsylvania Railroad* trains and wearing my Marine uniform with the FMD shoulder patch. Many civilians would come up to me and ask if I had been on Guadalcanal. When I answered "Yes" they would thank me, shake my hand, and even some women would hug and kiss me, which I really liked.

Another event which made this time of year special was the Thanksgiving Dinner they gave for us Marines at the Barracks. This was my first big holiday back stateside and had really missed the last two Turkey Days while I was away. Our Commanding Officer, Col. H. C. Pierce welcomed about 25 officers and 450 enlisted men to the dinner. This included the Chelsea, Squantum and South Boston Marine facilities as well as the main Boston Barracks. The fifteen cooks and bakers outdid themselves preparing the four course meal which included Turkeys from Vermont and Cranberry Sauce from Cape Cod. It was one of my best days as a Marine since the war started and I prayed that the war would be over by next Thanksgiving. Remembering all the good things that were my way of life here in America, I was slowly starting to heal from the loss I felt over my broken engagement with Jean and the reality of probably never seeing her again.

Another healing that was taking place in Boston was my return to regular medical treatments for the malaria and other jungle bacterium I had acquired in the jungles. There was concern that additional exposure occurred while in the New Guinea environs. Nearby our barracks was the first-rate Chelsea Naval Hospital which had some new protocols for veterans returning from the Pacific with these diseases. I was given regular blood tests to diagnose the status of the various parasites. They then administered newly developed antibiotic drugs to fight the bacteria, along with Atabrine or other specific quinine sulfates that had been developed. I felt blessed that they had this facility nearby for my needed treatments. This facility exceeded any of the other hospitals I had been to by far. It helped that I was no longer in a tropical climate and the colder weather would also aid in my recovery.

As we went about the day-to-day in Boston I tried to stay aware of what was happening with the FMD back in the Pacific. I received *Leatherneck* magazine and also read the papers and magazines including *The Saturday Evening Post*.

For Christmas 1944, I was able to get home just in time on Christmas Eve on a four day furlough and celebrate this special holiday with family. I was never more grateful that we were all together again. I prayed the war would end soon but knew first hand that the enemy we were up against would fight to the death as we clawed our way towards Tokyo.

Chapter 10

"V. J. DAY": August 14,1945

During the winter months of 1945 things at the barracks
ran pretty normal. It was my first winter in the NorthEast in
five years. The Marines had provided us with good wool
blankets and warm winter uniforms and I liked seeing the
snow again. In April, I took a mandatory exam and passed it
so I could still perform as the Supply Sergeant. We also
continued to practice and maintain our rifleman's status and
repeat *The Rifleman's Creed*. Back at the barracks, in early
May 1945, we got the terrific news that Germany had
surrendered unconditionally. The Navy Yard was still working
full steam ahead turning out ships and repairing others. The
threat of an attack from Europe had ended but now all eyes
turned to Japan. In the meantime, I was granted, by my
commanding officer, a furlough to return home for Mother's
Day for two whole weeks. They must have suspected we might
be called back to war duty in the Pacific sometime soon.

It was estimated that invading Japan could cost the lives
of one million US soldiers and airmen. Unfortunately those
would be many of our Marines. Based on the past experience
of the bloody island hoping campaigns, it was assumed that
Japan, once confronted at their own shores and cities, would
never surrender and would fight to the very last person. At
this time the FMD was still a force of twenty-thousand men

and certainly would have spearheaded the initial invasion and mostly likely been decimated. I fully expected that I would have been sent back for that ultimate battle. Fortunately, our President, Harry S. Truman, had the guts to drop the newly developed *A-bomb* which ended the war within a few days. The Emperor surrendered for the sake of his people and we celebrated in a major way all around the *Boston Commons*.

Honorable Discharge

It was never my plan to stay a Marine once the war ended. I had done enough and seen enough as one of the millions' of other *Citizen Soldiers*. Once Japan formally surrendered in Tokyo Bay on the deck of the battleship *USS Missouri* on 2 September 1945, it was my turn to be granted a discharge after 200 weeks of active duty. It took a little time for the paperwork to process and I still had lot's work as Supply Sergeant to wrap-up. The Marine Corps Muster Out Payroll policy required a discharge date to coincide with a month-end. My last paycheck was $100.80 for the month of October, plus five cents a mile for travel back to Philadelphia.

HONORABLE DISCHARGE: Staff Sergeant Wilbert Forrest West, Boston Navy Yard, October 31, 1945

On October 28th, my Dad wrote me a special letter. It captured the man he was; wise, faithful, a dry wit and a fan of Philadelphia's sports teams. He knew I would be coming home soon and penned these heartfelt words:

Personally, I feel we have much to be thankful, that you have come through all ordeals safely. I trust upon your return to civilian life, you will meet with the success, you fellas who have sacrificed so much time in service, deserve. So my boy, farewell to your Marine activities, and the best of luck again for all your future.

Lovingly Dad

So, I did return to civilian life starting November 1, 1945. I was no longer a *Leatherneck* in phrase, but once a Marine you were always a Marine. We would always be reverently referred to as: "The Old Breed of American Regulars."

"We were the old-timers, our rifles and bayonets were high and holy things to worship and after many battles in the jungles and islands, the war became our occupation," as stoically written by John Thomason, Jr in *Fix Bayonets*.

James Michener, the author, wrote these special words at the end of the first chapter in his *Tales of The South Pacific:*

"They will live a long time, these men of the South Pacific. They had an American quality. They, like their victories, will be remembered as long as our generation lives. After that... longer and longer shadows will obscure them, until Guadalcanal sounds distant on the ear like Shiloh and Valley Forge."

Chapter 11

Epilogue from the Son: Dad's Story

Ever since I did a forty page high school term report on *The War in the Pacific*, complete with maps and illustrations, I have been interested in knowing more about my Dad's Marine Corps experiences. At home there had been copies of old *Leatherneck* magazines, a brochure on Camp Lejeune and other assorted materials from his WWII days he let me look at. But he never provided much of an oral history. He helped me with the report, but only the mechanics of putting it together, not the contents. Over the years, I sought out other details from him, like where else was he during the War? I did get some small facts out of him about the time in New Guinea, and the Boston Navy Yard, but never enough to completely satisfy my curiosity. When he passed away in 1993, I was in mid-career. It wasn't until my retirement two decades later, that I could devote the time and travel to learn on my own what his Marine experience was all about.

Valor Tour to Guadalcanal

In August 2011, Uncle Walt and I went on a long anticipated military tour to the Solomon Islands for two weeks. We had the noted Guadalcanal historian, John Innes, as our preeminent guide, and along with about 35 others, got to see first hand all the historic battle sites as well as participate in the 69th Anniversary of the Guadalcanal landings on 7 August. This was held at *The American Memorial* site high above the coast. There was also the American Ambassador, a contingent of active duty Marines with Band members and dignitaries from many countries in attendance that gave commemorative speeches.

Wreaths placed by many of the National Dignitaries at Memorial.

One of the highlights that day was personally dedicating two plaques in *The Memorial Garden of Honor* just outside Henderson Field. One came from my Uncle and the other was from Mom, Deborah and myself. Each one was placed at the base of a unique slender tree, called a *Carallia Brachiata*.

Dad's Memorial Tree - It is in a Peaceful Grove of reflection.

(LETTER READ AND LEFT AT DAD'S TREE DEDICATION)

Wilbert "Bill" Forrest West, First Marine Division "The Old Breed"
Guadalcanal - August 7th 1942 to December 9th 1942

Staff Sergeant West, who landed here on this day sixty-nine years ago was part of the "Greatest Generation" who endured the Great Depression, helped defeat Imperial Japan and then quietly returned home to build a better life. After the war, as did many other veterans; he married, raised a family and lived the rest of his days in his hometown until his death in 1993. He hardly ever spoke about what happened on this island, only the occasional tidbit or acknowledgment, but that's ok because the history has now been documented which makes their actions here immortal.

My father was everything I would want to be. Good, moral, decent, hard working, very humble and loved his country.

This trip and tree planting has finally brought us here to honor him and provide a lasting tribute to the sacrifice he made with his fellow Marines.

David Forrest West   August 7, 2011

Research, Reading & Reminiscing

Coming home from that tour I started to do a lot more research. For $60 I was able to obtain a copy of my Father's complete military file from the government's central record facility in St. Louis. That gave me an enormous amount of data on his complete movements including ship names. I also pulled together, from his saved personal records, that my Mother had kept, a lot of other pieces of the puzzle. In my free time I read as much as I could on Guadalcanal and the Marines. I also watched the HBO mini-series *The Pacific.* I began getting connected with other history buffs and finding out about Veteran Groups that, although in their twilight years, still held reunions. I joined the *Guadalcanal Veterans Association* (GVA) and attended several of their reunions around the country until they ceased being active in 2016. The Veterans that were still able to attend, many on walkers and wheelchairs, gave me a lot of insight during those events. I treasured the times during the informal "bull sessions." Mostly in their nineties, they had now all opened up about their war experience and supplied many unvarnished stories of the "real skinny" back then. The GVA newsletters also provided some insights. *The FMD Association* has an active group that I became an associate member of after proving my relationship and began getting their newsletter; *The Old Breed News.* I am also a proud member of *The Southern Cross Team* a special donor group within this association.

Family Letters Provide Clues? Yes and No!

Part of putting the puzzle together were the personal letters that Dad had kept and brought back home from his family and friends. His mother wrote the most of course, but his Father wrote a lot of times with informative news from *The Home Front.* Somehow I had always thought there must have been letters saved that he had written. If there were any, they probably were kept by Aunt Mildred and passed on to my Uncle. During one evening at The Mendana Hotel in Honiara, I asked Walt if he knew of any letters written by my Dad during the war. He said there might be some in a storage locker. I impressed upon him how important they would be for his children to get those letters back. Eventually he turned a stack of them over to my sister in 2013 before he passed away in 2016. But he also said there were three other envelopes, with typed letters written in early 1944 addressed to Mildred at her work address that were; "too personal of family matters" for us to have. Eventually, all I got was the empty envelope. Walt must have tried to protect something, but why these many years later? We are the grown children and should know about these "family matters." This was far beyond disappointing because I believe it would have given us clues as to what had happened in Melbourne with Jean. Combine that secrecy with Dad's somewhat veiled comment to me when I first travelled to Melbourne in 1973 for a three month work assignment. He said matter of factly; "Son, don't

Final Salute in my "Dress Blues" Semper Fi

be surprised if you see someone down there that looks like you." Those were his exact words and to this day I regret not asking what he meant or seeking a way to find out while in Melbourne. Could my Sister and I actually have had a half-sibling that would be five years older than me? I believe so.

The Final Duty Station for this Marine

My Father passed away on 17 February 1993 at age 74. For the last decade of his life he had suffered from the effects of Parkinson's disease. I have to believe this was partly a result of the many chemical imbalances in his system from the jungle diseases he was afflicted with during the war. He also suffered the various effects of malaria and blood disorders for many years while never complaining. This was just always his way, never complain and never explain.

He had a strong belief in *God and Country* and faithfully served in our Presbyterian Church as an Elder. As a boy, I would sit next to him in that church on most Sundays. He always devoted the first several minutes with his head bowed, eyes closed in silent prayer. I believe those prayers were to keep his commitment to honor his fellow Marines and to grieve for the souls of those heroes that did not make it home to experience their life into adulthood as he had been blessed.

I also believe that when he entered *The Pearly Gates* he announced his arrival shouting: "Marine Bill West reporting to my Final Duty Station. I have served my time in Hell."

Finally, How to Tell Dad's Story?

At the beginning of 2018, realizing my Father would have been 100 years old in 2019, I decided to pull together all that I had uncovered and began writing this memoir so that I could present it to the family during his Centennial Birth Year.

I chose this style of writing, in the first person narrative, as I imagined my Dad would've said things during that era. I also wanted it to be relatable to the next generations. In order to fully document this period of his personal history, I decided I would take some author's prerogative by adding conjecture and perhaps a bit of colorful imagination to fill in the gaps where there were little or no details to fall back on. However, the vast majority of this written memoir comes from a foundation of documented research over many years from hard historical facts; including names, dates and times.

I wanted this memoir to be told as a tale worth telling and with a truly believable storyline which will stand as an other testament to the legend of *The US Marine Corps*.

I hope that it succeeded.

Semper Fidelis Dad. We've got the Watch.

David Forrest West

BILL WEST - STAFF SERGEANT
FIRST MARINE DIVISION - REINFORCED
AUGUST 7 - DECEMBER 9, 1942
"THE OLD BREED"

Plaque at base of his tree on Guadalcanal

Today there are still many ways to learn about and keep the history of Guadalcanal and World War II alive. A few museums and memorials come to mind:

- The World War II National Museum in New Orleans, LA

- The Marine Corps Museum in Quantico, VA

- The WWII Memorial in Washington, DC

- The National Museum of the Pacific War in Texas

- The Annual John Basilone Parade in Raritan, NJ

- August 7 th Memorial Ceremony on Guadalcanal with Valor

- FMD Headquarters at Marine Corps Base in Pendelton, CA

- Arlington National Cemetery, Arlington, VA

Back Cover

WW II Memorial in Washington D.C.